Win with China

I0468710

A Bite-Sized Business Book

# Acclimatisation for Mutual Success

## Doing Business with China

Ma Maiqi

Published by Bite-Sized Books Ltd 2016

Published by:

Bite-Sized Books Ltd
Cleeve Croft, Cleeve Road, Goring RG8 9BJ UK
information@bite-sizedbooks.com
Registered in the UK. Company Registration No: 9395379

# Contents

# Introduction
## Will My China Dream Come True?

*China is ancient, yet she is modern; she has illness, yet she is vibrant; she is worrisome, yet she is soothing; it is the place where the nightmare begins, yet it is the place where my dream comes true...' (Hi, I am China)*

This first hand introduction to doing business in China will introduce you not only to some of the steps you need to take to win with China but more importantly to how you will be perceived and how you will need to act and conduct yourself in order to be successful.

China has the second largest economy in the world, yet she also has the biggest population living in poverty (600million in 2015); the Chinese have become the world's No. 1 luxury consumers, yet China has the greatest gap between rich and poor (China's GINI index was 0.42 in 2005, the world average was 0.4). Big contrast means big opportunities, or growth space. Jack Ma of Alibaba said, 'When all of the Chinese people have Internet, I can build another Alibaba.' Such an emerging economy is becoming a dreamland for much western business expansion. However big opportunities are often twinned with big risks. As the Chinese say, 'At any time, there is always someone ecstatic while someone else is left miserable.'

The most recognised challenges of doing business in China for westerners are:

- Getting paid
- Higher starting costs
- Chinese law and regulations
- Cultural differences
- Communication with Chinese people
- Market potential
- Intellectual property protection
- Natural resources
- Political risks (including financial and international treaties)
- Labour quality and labour costs
- Local competitors

- The change of personal life
- Technology
- Corruption
- Bureaucracy

But hang on a minute: if I said that all of these challenges are the same as those Chinese business people face, would you believe it? According to a survey by the Chinese magazine 'Scientific Investment', the average lifespan of Chinese Small and Medium Enterprises (SMEs) is 3-4 years. On the other hand, in 2014, foreign businesses contributed about 10% of China's GDP, equivalent to 1,035,483 million USD.

Compared to Chinese business people, their foreign competitors enjoy some advantages. People say, 'It is easier for a foreign monk to recite scriptures.' Why? Because most Chinese people have a 'western worship', that is western culture, ideas and technology are widely admired and embraced. Also, people tend to be more tolerant of foreigners. For example, if you try to speak Mandarin with Chinese colleagues and get the pronunciation wrong, they will happily and politely correct you, and genuinely appreciate your efforts. But if this happened with a Chinese person, they would mock him or her for having 'no culture'.

So, to do business in China successfully, challenges are present not only for foreigners, but also for Chinese people. The distinction is that we will each face varying degrees of difficulty in different aspects. In this book, you will discover both your advantages and disadvantages, and how to build on those advantages and mitigate the disadvantages. And of course, common sense considerations also have a role to play.

Chinese people say that three factors are needed to successfully accomplish a project: the right time, right place and right people. You will find out here whether now is the right time for you to expand into China, where in China is the right place for you and how you can find the right people to work with.

This book will be useful to as a reference and a guide. It will help you to avoid commonly encountered pitfalls and cultural faux pas and to navigate through red tape, but of course the road to success will ultimately depend on you.

Enjoy and good luck!

# Chapter 1
## Getting Ready for China – Who Am I and Who Are They?

Whatever your motivation for wanting to enter or expand into China, you should ask yourself these questions: Who am I? What I am doing? Why do I want to go to China? Am I emotionally and physically fit enough to live there and commute between my home country and China? How can I get on well with Chinese people? What are my advantages and disadvantages? How much can I afford to lose, in time or money? If I'm successful, how successful do I want to be? Here, all of these 'I's can of course, also be 'we's.

You should also ask: who are they (the Chinese)? Do they need my products or services? How can I get them to like me, my products and services? How much are they willing to pay? How many of them (or much of it) can they afford to buy?

All these questions, in professional terms, are about one's personal, social and cultural identity. You can find the answers by self-assessment, making friends with Chinese people and by consulting with professionals. If you are confident enough, make a trip to China, live with the local people, eat with them, talk to them, listen to them and observe them empathetically. 'If you want to know the taste of a pear, you should have a bite.'

After nearly ten years living, studying and doing business in the UK, I am not only more or less Anglicised (organised, patient and rational), which allows me to get on well with the British; but I'm also getting more and more clear about what made me Chinese (Daoism and Confucianism). I equally love both countries and am aware of what I value in both.

This utterly exceeded my expectations. Why? Because when I decided to leave China for the UK, I thought that I would have a better life; plus earning GB pounds wouldn't be a bad thing (£1≈ ¥15 in 2008). But my optimism was fleeting. Feeling like 'a fish out of water', the UK was like an 'open prison' for me. Cultural isolation affected me mentally and physically: I suffered from insomnia and hair loss.

After my business expansion dream burst (no big surprise, it was at the time that the recession began) I went job hunting. Smartly dressed, confident and enthusiastic, roaming around all kinds of job fairs and agency offices, I never once got a job offer. Until, one day, I received a phone call from a lady. She said, 'It's very interesting to read your CV. But to be honest, I have piles and piles of CVs: all the applicants are very experienced and many have a PhD qualification. Your problem is that you don't have any UK qualifications or working background...'

To this day I'm still grateful to this lady. She persuaded me to ask myself, 'Who am I?' Well, I'm a Chinese, and that is my disadvantage in competing with Britons. I have a Chinese education and business background: how can I use it?

The answer? I'm going to sell these skills to the British. It worked! Now even multi-billion pound corporations are using my services! In China we say: 'The place where you fall should be where you stand tall.'

Normally, people from western countries have many more advantages than those from developing countries. This is often because of the better education in the west. Chinese people call working or studying abroad 'to gild yourself overseas'. To deal with China be prepared to expect the unexpected. China and the Chinese people are different to what you'll have seen or heard in your home country. When I had just arrived in the UK, I felt that all westerners looked similar. Nowadays, I can not only tell how distinctive they are, but am also able to distinguish many kinds of regional accents and personality traits. It will similarly take time to develop your own insight by getting involved in people's lives and understanding their history, culture and philosophy.

Speaking of differences, it is worth listening to how Chinese people describe life in the west and China respectively, 'So clean, so beautiful and so lonely; so dirty, so messy and so happy.' What does this imply then?

Let's firstly leave aside our human similarities as set out in Maslow's 'Hierarchy of Needs', and consider our differences.

What makes Chinese people happy? Human affection! The strong attachment to one another. When Chinese people come to the west they very often find that it is very lonely, and that although westerners may be friendly, it is hard to make real friends. They miss the constant interaction with family, friends and colleagues that is so much a part of Chinese life and culture, such as frequent social gatherings, meals and gift giving.

Here are some major comparisons: western individualism v. Chinese collectivism; western rationality v. Chinese emotions; western abstraction v. Chinese intuition; western convergent thinking v. Chinese divergent thinking. These topics can go really deep and far. But let me give you just one example.

You know how different Mandarin Chinese is from your mother tongue? Good! Let's take it a little bit further.

Mandarin is primarily a picture based language, while alphabetic languages are sound based. When we mentally process our languages, we are using different part of our brains. Now you know one of the reasons why there are so many communication breakdowns between us. We think in different ways!

Some notable fundamental differences between Chinese and western values are: in Chinese culture, morality is valued over utility and intelligence; family, group or a country are more important than an individual; peace and harmony are valued over conflict and liberty; spiritual nobility over substance.

You may also have heard lots about Chinese focus on 'Relationship', 'Face' and 'Hierarchy'. Are you a little bit scared because you don't know how to deal with hierarchy? Well, I hate it that some people overstate these concepts and take them out of context. Someone once told me that he was hosting a Chinese business delegation of mixed gender, age and position. He concentrated his attentions on one of the delegates, whom he assumed to be senior, enthusiastically introducing his business and working place. At the end, he belatedly realised that this person was only a junior member of the entourage, and did not take any of his words in.

See how natural it is for us to pay more attention to someone that we assume is more important!

What is the best approach then? Equally welcome everyone, introduce yourself and your team, ask them to introduce themselves. If you don't know how to arrange the seating, leave it to them, and observe attentively without assumption.

You will soon find out who is the senior and most respected, then you can focus on them. If you show more respect to the elderly and to ladies in the first instance, it won't be wrong. If you want to know more about them, just ask. The word 'knowledge' in Chinese literally combines 'learn' and 'ask'. 'Asking' is a manifestation of modesty and 'studiousness', and it is a virtuous attainment.

In fact, Chinese people don't use 'hierarchy' to describe our society. We differentiate between seniors and juniors, and recognise priority in rank, but the Chinese order is led by harmony, including family values, collective consciousness, sharing and tolerance.

If you want to get on well with Chinese people, you will have to make a psychological journey: be clearly aware of who you are, but then readjust your outlook and behaviour to be more like one of them. If you can manage this, then you won't be a stranger to them, and after a while it will become natural to you.

# Chapter 2
Is China right for me? Chinese policies for foreign investors
If you are bright, China will never be dark.

Before you take the plunge and enter the Chinese business arena it's important to be aware of how Chinese government policies will affect your particular business area. Depending on your product or service these effects can range from troublesome but minor to completely show stopping, so do make sure that you research thoroughly before you commit too much of your time and money. I will give you guidance on the main considerations in this chapter.

Firstly, trade restrictions can apply in all areas and industries. As an example, ten years ago, I was having dinner with two representatives of the Australian Trade Commission in Guangzhou. They disclosed that they were negotiating with the Chinese government to allow Australian seafood products into the Chinese market. I asked, "But where are those 'Australian Lobsters' from? They're ¥ 800 per half kilo in the local market." "We don't know. But clearly none of them is legally imported from Australia." they replied. In fact, the lobsters in question were being falsely advertised as Australian in order to raise the price (and of course increase the trader's profits).

In 2015, a China / Australia Free Trade Agreement was reached. When real Australian lobsters landed in China, thanks to the advance publicity gained from their fake compatriots, the retailers saved big sums of money on marketing and branding. When they displayed real Australian lobsters in their original packaging, people flocked to their counters.

So, in international business, not only do local market trends need to be investigated, but also political sensitivity is absolutely crucial. Did you know, that many Chinese companies have a division called 'Policy Research Department'?

The main reason for this is the Chinese government's flexible and changeable policy attitudes, including central and regional macro-controls and micro-regulations, and administrative interventions such as Local Protection (which may be either reasonable or unreasonable).

Remember too that China is a developing country, the GDP per capita in 2015 was US$7,990, world ranking 73. Because of this, poor infrastructure in many areas means that information channels aren't well developed and hardware facilities may be obsolescent or simply not in place.

As the largest ruling party in the world, with huge geographic and ethnic cultural disparities and bordering on 21 countries, the Chinese central government has always been challenged by extremely complex international and domestic situations. In order to maintain state stability and balance, industrial restructuring and regional adjustment is a must. And yet, the Chinese Communist Party has only been in power since 1949 and are still not old hands at government.

Another stumbling block can be the Chinese personality trait of ambiguous expression. A Chinese economist pointed out that there are many 'language corruptions' in Chinese official documents. It is so true! I once attended a 'Revenue and Tax Explanation Seminar' presented by a 'Central Leader' from Beijing. Afterwards, there were many questions from confused delegates. The presenter was forced to admit that, 'At top level, explanations are unclear, so at the bottom people cannot understand at all.' In Chinese literature, we often hear that an idea 'can only be intuited, but cannot be articulated.' That is why Chinese people often eulogise Germanic exactitude in language.

All that said, the Chinese government is committed to being more open: a relatively recent initiative toward this end was the launch in 2013 of the China (Shanghai) Pilot Free Trade Zone.

The Chinese government at all levels is hungry for foreign investment, and there are specialised government departments whose role is to attract foreign investors. There are also specialised departments to assist overseas Chinese in visiting, working and investing in China. However, my research indicates that very few foreigners are aware of these favourable policies towards them, and that most 'Foreign Investment' in China continues to be from Hong Kong, Taiwan or overseas Chinese.

There are some paramount guidelines for consideration before first entering China: thorough market research is essential; prospective business partners in China must be carefully assessed and cultural awareness and sensitivity is of enormous importance, (do not underestimate this aspect!).

In particular, you need to be aware of the Chinese government's policy of favoured, restricted and prohibited industries for foreign investors.

There are as many as 349 categories in 12 industries that have been listed as favoured investments. This means that investment in these areas will enjoy simplified approval procedures, national and international funding and loans, land leasing, taxation deduction, social publicity and so on.

Restricted industries encompass 38 categories in all. The restrictions mean prescriptive limitations on share-holdings between Chinese undertakings and foreign investors. Additionally, involvement in other industries may be limited by international treaties concluded by or acceded to by the Chinese government.

Prohibited industries include the media, national infrastructure and defence, and of course vice (although this last probably goes without saying!).

However, even in the prohibited industries area exceptions may be made: for example, the nuclear industry is one which is in general prohibited to foreigners. Notwithstanding this, China's emergent (and burgeoning) nuclear industry has relied very heavily on foreign involvement, with Areva (France) acting as a major partner in new reactor build and commercial power reactor fuel fabrication.

Indicative lists of these industries are presented for your guidance in Appendix A, but do be aware that these are not exhaustive, and that they are subject to change.

## References:
Ministry of Commerce of the People's Republic of China - http://www.mofcom.gov.cn
http://english.mofcom.gov.cn

## Favoured Industries, Restricted Industries, Prohibited Industries
### Favoured industries

New agricultural technology; Comprehensive agricultural development; Renewable energy; Transportation; Raw material industrial projects; High-tech projects; Exporting; Comprehensive utilization of resources and renewable resources; Pollution preventing projects; Industrial transformation; projects that can bring socio-economic benefits to inner China (especially central and western region), and labour-intensive projects.

## Restricted industries

These include agriculture, forestry, livestock, fisheries, mining, manufacturing, energy and water, information, software, wholesale and retail, finance, leasing and business services, science research and technology services, health care and social services, education, culture, sport and entertainment,

## Prohibited industries

Research and development, breeding and cultivation of China's listed precious breeds; Transgenic breeding and seeding; Aquatic fishing; exploration and mining of tungsten, molybdenum, tin, antimony, fluorite, rare earth and radioactive minerals, listed Chinese traditional medicine production; radioactive minerals, nuclear fuel and weapon processing; ivory carving, tiger bone processing; Xuan paper and ink ingot production; Within large power grid, construction and operation of stand-alone capacity of 300,000 kilowatts or below coal-fired condensing thermal power station, stand-alone capacity of 200,000 kilowatts coal-fired condensing steam extraction and dual-use cogeneration power plant; Air Traffic Control; Post and domestic express mail service; Wholesale or retail in tobacco, cigarettes and other tobacco products; Social survey; Chinese Legal Advisory; Human stem cells, gene diagnosis and treatment technology development and applications; Geodesy, mapping and geological survey; Nature reserves and wetlands construction and operation; Protected wildlife's development; Compulsory education; Military, police and political institutions and other special educational organisations; News agency; Publications (books, newspaper, magazine, audio and video products and electronic publications); Broadcasting, TV station and channels; Radio and television program production company; Film production and distribution companies, cinema companies; News sites, online publishing, internet audio-visual program services, Internet access service and the internet cultural business (except music); Auction business involves in cultural relics, and antique shops; Golf course and villa construction; Endanger the safety and performance of military facilities projects, Gambling industry and Porn industry.

# Chapter 3

Where is my niche in China? Going there, living with the people, listening to them,

You can never find truth by poking one eye out. (Zhou Xiaoping)

Having decided to enter the Chinese market, one of your first questions is, "Where should I locate in China?". In this chapter, we will discuss how to find the ideal place for your business.

I was once at a 'Doing business in China' event organised by a large, UK government funded body. It took place in a nice venue: the food was good, the presentations were well delivered and exciting business opportunities in China were described.

At the end, the organisers revealed their mission, to persuade delegates to join a business tour to Guangdong (a southern province in China).

An English gentleman sitting next to me wondered whether he could meet potential business partners if he joined the trip. When I asked him about his business area, he gave me his card; the company marketed agricultural machinery. I said to him, 'Guangdong is not for you, they will be interested in industrial machinery. Guangdong is the manufactory of world, but there's not much farmland.'

As you probably know, China is a vast country, it has the world's largest population and third biggest land area. But often, I have to say, 'You need to think even bigger.

Form a 3D view, imagine the terrain. China rises in altitude from east to west: Lhasa is 3,656 metres above sea level, while Shanghai is just 4 metres. There are people living on a vast plateau above 4,000 metres, where the children have no idea what apples look like. Also imagine the variation in temperature and humidity: in winter, the temperature difference between north and south can be up to 60°C. It is deadly dry in the north west, but stickily humid in the south east.

The geographic and climactic variations result in not only in biodiversity, but also in cultural and industrial diversity.

In China the common administrative divisions are:

- Provinces of which there are twenty-two
- Autonomous Regions (Guangxi Zhuang, Inner Mongolia, Tibet, Ningxia Hui, Xinjiang Uygur), Municipalities (Beijing, Tianjin, Shanghai and Chongqing)
- Special Administrative Regions (Hong Kong and Macau).

However, there is an extreme imbalance from region to region. For example, Xinjiang accounts for about one-sixth of China's land area, but only 0.15% of the total Chinese population and 1.3% GDP, while Guangdong province at only 1.87% by land area, with 0.86% of the population contributes almost 11% of China's total GDP (in 2015). Therefore, in practice, there are many other ways of zoning China in terms of the economy, political sensitivities, religion, culture and numerous other aspects.

Historically, there were three main economic 'Dragon Heads': the Yangtze River Delta (major city Shanghai), the Pearl River Delta (major city Guangzhou) and Bohai Bay (major cities Beijing and Tianjin). Benefiting from convenient water transport by sea and river, these east coastal regions have relatively mature commercial markets and good human resources; however, the competition here is also more intense.

In order to balance the gap between east and west, the Chinese central government initiated the 'Rise of Central China', 'Revitalise Northeast China' and 'Reinvigorate

China Western Development' strategies. The specific actions included approving Chongqing's municipality status in 1997, and free Border Trading treaties.

Affected by historical, geographical and other aspects, each city or region possesses distinctive attributes and characteristics. For instance, Shanghai is twinned with 70 cities and regions across the globe. Needless to say Shanghai is the most international city in China. It is the centre of the financial, services and fashion industries in China, extending its influence across all of Asia. Chongqing is a rising star in all aspects, while Harbin is claimed to be the 'Oriental Moscow'.

Undoubtedly, lifestyle and personalities are also very different. We say, 'Shanghainese dare to wear anything, Beijingers dare to say anything, and Cantonese dare to eat anything'. 'If your flight lands in Chengdu at midnight, you will hear people playing 'Majiang' (a Chinese board game played by 4 people), if you land in Guangzhou at midnight, you will be able to find an open restaurant.'

The regional diversity is such that many ethnic minorities and regions appear 'foreign' even to the majority of other Chinese!

Attitudes towards business? Of course these differ too. We say, 'If a Shanghainese has one dollar, he would save 50 cents, and invest 50 cents; if a Cantonese has one dollar, he would borrow 1 dollar and invest 2 dollars. And how about the Beijingers? They will probably just spend it all on friends.

It is easy to see that Shanghainese are savvy, whereas the Cantonese are more laid back: their attitude is; 'there is money for all of us to earn, I am satisfied with what I have got, I don't mind if you earn more than me.' They are my favourite business partners.

It is worth noting that flight time from Guangzhou to Beijing is three hours and ten minutes, and, for many businesses, managing their regional agencies can be a major challenge. Considering the costs, most SMEs choose indirect multiple level distribution channels. Commonly, the first level will be the seven geographical divisions: North China, Northeast China, East China, Central China, South China, Northwest China and Southwest China. At the second level are the provinces, then the administrative regions, then the counties. Some products will need agents at the final level, boroughs. Because of the density of population and physical distances, these may well beyond your reach. In the fight for market share, price wars among the agencies are commonplace. The result? Potential damage to your brand.

Therefore, the challenge is not only where to locate, but also how to deploy your distribution centres and manage the channels.

To answer the question of the English gentleman mentioned earlier: to market his agricultural machinery he should go to China's granary, the Sanjiang Plain in the northeast, or to the Jianghan Plain in Hubei province; dubbed the 'land of fish and rice'.

In conclusion, in deciding where to locate, you need consider many factors including living costs (Shanghai is expensive!), life style, natural resources, transport, communications, human resources (including English language proficiency), climate (look at the incidence of natural disasters; floods, earthquakes and typhoons), the commercial environment, regional influences, cultural diversity, central and local politics and policies.

If you intend to relocate to China in person in the medium to long term (two to five plus years) and to take your family with you then you must also consider factors such as schooling, medical care, proficiency in Chinese, cultural adjustment and homesickness. Obviously you should also take some of these into account for yourself.

Take it from me, culture shock can be very hard to come to terms with, so don't just assume that you'll be able to cope!

# Chapter 4
## Choosing a Business Entity

If your business is in one of China's favoured categories and you have found the right location for expansion, the next step is to choose an entity. In this chapter I will start by giving some examples to illustrate the different approaches.

In the early 1980s the courier companies DHL, UPS, TNT and FEDEX were all aiming for a share of the Chinese market. At that time, all foreign courier services were obliged to cooperate with China's state owned SINOTRANS. Overseas business was handled entirely by the foreign companies, with SINOTRANS being responsible for the majority of domestic operations. DHL was the first company to sign a mutual agency agreement with SINOTRANS, that was in 1980.

In 1986, Chinese policy changed. Foreign couriers could now enter into a joint venture in China, but the highest permitted capital investment ratio was 50%. Consequently, DHL and SINOTRANS established a 50:50 joint venture, the agreed contract period for which was 50 years.

This was followed in 1988 by agreements between UPS-SINOTRANS and SINOTRANS–TNT. In contrast FEDEX retained its mutual agency status with SINOTRANS, but all three entered into 15 year contractual periods.

In December 2001, China entered the WTO. According to the treaty, international freight forwarding companies could hold a 75% investment ratio during the period 2001 to 2005. Following this they were permitted to register as a Wholly Foreign Owned Enterprise (WFOE).

In 2003, TNT discontinued its joint venture contract with SINOTRANS, followed by UPS in 2005. Chinese pundits call this 'Forced marriage' and 'Chinese style divorce'. The 'divorce' cost UPS 100 million USD, but gave UPS an established business and operations network in more than 200 Chinese cities. SINOTRANS staff lamented that they had acted as 'super salesman' for UPS. TNT acquired China's largest private road freight company for 135 million USDs.

FEDEX resisted 'marriage' to the communist party's company, and chose a private Chinese partner, DTW, in 1999. Later, in 2005, it acquired DTW's whole business at a cost of 400 million USDs. This move 'coincided' with the release of China's seventh draft Postal Law which removed a number of restrictions on foreign companies' activities and significantly increased FEDEX's business scope within China.

Currently, only SINOTRANS – DHL are still 'married'. The partnership has benefited from the advantages offered by policy changes, with an average annual business growth of 40%, revenue rises of 6000%, and its market share in China increasing to 37%. This is a great example of a rare international 'happy marriage'. Mr Xu, CEO of DHL Express said, 'We run the business through a cooperative attitude, not a rigid concept.' While Mr Zhao, CEO of SINOTRANS said, 'Communication is vital.'

By the way, although somewhat overshadowed by the SINTOTRANS – DHL success story, it's important to note that UPS, TNT and FEDEX haven't done badly. All have seen a very respectable business growth rate of greater than 20% per annum.

This case is typical, same business, same partner, same policy, but different stories. After all, the choice is in your hands. It also shows that the influencing factors are varied and changeable.

From simple to complex, foreign companies are able to choose an arrangement that best suits their need. They may set up a Representative Office, engage with a Chinese company in a Small Share Joint Venture, Equal Share Joint Venture or Holding Joint Venture, or they may set up as a Wholly Foreign Owned Enterprise (WFOE).

Depending on the degree of openness to foreign investments for your particular industry, (set by Chinese government policy as explained in Chapter 2), and your company's capital, marketing power and product compatibility, you can select your preferred entity type. Generally speaking, if openness and capabilities are both high, then a WFOE is the better bet.

If you choose a joint venture, having the 'right' partner is absolutely crucial. The first consideration will be whether to choose a state owned company or private company. The advantage of a state owned company is that they own any land, and that they are better informed. The main disadvantage will be from the inevitable political maneuvering, both internal and external. Again, you need think about it carefully and thoroughly.

Different types of entity have different registration procedures, and different regions have different approaches. Don't expect that it can all be done online, and all at once. The process can be extremely confusing and cumbersome. You really need someone knowledgeable (and trustworthy) to do everything in person.

The costs are relatively high, and don't be surprised at hidden fees. For example, companies are required to display all relevant registration certificates at their premises. You may well find yourself compelled to buy your certificates mounted in cheap frames but at enormously inflated prices! The provision by you of gifts and entertainment will be expected, and are the norm. The size of the gifts depends on the region, business type, the size and difficulty level, and will range from hundreds to thousands of Renminbi. Do bear in mind though that China's government is engaged in a crackdown on corruption, and you must be careful not to cross the line between hospitality and bribery! So, where's the line in the sand? Hospitality and gifts up to a total of 5,000 Renminbi are permitted; if you stray over the boundary you're committing a criminal offence.

The documents needed for foreign company registration are:

1. Company name pre-registration (Application form, proof of investors' legal status, Power of Attorney of Registration and other papers).
2. Opening Registration (Application form signed by the Legal Representative, Contract, Articles of Association, Approval documents and Certificate of Approval, Proof of Investors' status, Proof of investors' Credit Certificate, List of Directors and managers, Identity, Proof of residence and premises, Project proposals and approval documents and other papers).

That's not all, there's much, much more to be done, Taxation, the Labour and Social Security Bureau and so on. The easiest way to proceed is to go to one of the government offices and ask where you can find an agent to do all these things for you: it's very likely that you'll find one nearby. Do engage them: although it will cost you some money it'll save you lots of time and trouble. It's an open secret that these agency businesses are normally owned by the officials' relatives.

If you can open the door for your business in four months, well done you! What should you realistically allow? I would recommend 6-18 months depending on the business type.

Now, let's talk about your company name. You will have to have a Chinese name for your company in China. A good name is half way to success. The State Administration for Industry & Commerce of the People's Republic of China has restrictions for company names. Over and above this, you need think about whether it is memorable and meaningful. Chinese people are superstitious; a good meaning is essential.

So far, Coca-Cola is still the biggest winner with their Chinese name. They have chosen 可口可乐, in Chinese Pinyin (Pinyin is the standard Romanised spelling system for Chinese) this is 'Ke Kou Ke Le'. How ingenious is it? Well, the first two characters together mean 'delicious', while the second two characters mean 'joyful'. And, the sounds are so similar that they are easy to pronounce for all Chinese people. The other one that I like is Mercedes-Benz, their Chinese name is 奔驰, (Pinyin 'Ben Chi'). It sounds reasonably similar to "Benz" in the original, and the two characters form a common Chinese word meaning to run quickly or gallop.

When choosing a Chinese name, the sound, meaning and pinyin version all need to be taken into account. There was a Chinese toilet roll brand, the Chinese characters for which mean poetic and graceful. However, the Pinyin Romanisation as it appeared on the package was 'Shi ting'. From an English speaker's perspective this conveys very little in the way of grace or poetry! They are not alone, and even native English speakers can make silly mistakes. For example: 'Counselling California' originally chose the domain name of 'www.therapistfinder.com'. They subsequently changed the name to 'www.counsellingcalifornia.com'), doubtless after no little measure of embarrassment. While these are certainly memorable it's probably true to say that the reasons we remember them are not those the organisations intended! A quick web search will reveal many more such examples, some apocryphal, but others only too real.

Take care, in China good luck starts with a good name! I would suggest that you pick one that implies good wishes and sounds similar to your native one but not simply a transliteration. It's probably best that you take advice from a Chinese professional when choosing your name.

# Chapter 5
## Managing Complex Business Relationships in China

My personal experience is that managing relationships is a big part of business life in China. If you can make and maintain good relationships, it will save you lots of effort and allow you to achieve better results.

The first day that I went to kindergarten in China, my parents and grandparents said to me with deep earnestness, "Listen to the teachers, and build a good relationship with them, and with the other 'little friends'". These words were repeated again and again until I started my career, '...build a good rapport with your leaders and colleagues...' In practice, this means to be considerate, to proactively do good deeds, to share and to bear difficulties.

When I started my business adventure, I benefited immensely from this ethos because it helped me to make friends and expand my social network. However, to sustain healthy, long term, all-around relationships can be extremely exhausting. Business social intercourse not only means gift giving, banquets and entertaining, but sometimes also descends into the world of vice, with sex, gambling and drugs being offered as inducements. When dealing with government institutions especially, being able to bribe in a discreet way became a much-sought-after skill. However, as noted in Chapter 4, the Chinese government is actively engaged in trying to root out graft in its 'Tigers and Flies' (i.e. big and small) anti-corruption drive. How then to win favour for yourself and your business without falling foul of the authorities? There are many ways to get round this, such as supporting local education and sponsoring socio-economic projects to raise your publicity and enhance your reputation.

Many years later, when I undertook a National Occupational training course in the UK, I was taught about 'boundaries' at work, and to 'be friendly, but your colleagues are not your friends'. Although I knew a little bit about western 'privacy', it was still nerve-racking. It was true that I was weary of China's complex web of relationships, but I did not expect, or want to be, a smiling 'cold fish' either.

Interestingly, I have seen a reverse of these dogmas, especially when I got involved in a UK based global leadership coaching business in 2015. A group of senior Leaders and Shapers urge corporate chiefs to build trusted relationships with their staff. A typical example came from a store executive in the John Lewis organisation. Before the store opens in the morning, he greets the staff in front of the entrance with friendly chitchat such as: 'How is everyone in your family?'

On the other hand, in traditionally collective China, a society of complex, interwoven relationships, etiquette and favour, the new outlook is; 'Business is business; even fathers and sons should distinguish between their profits'. This is being stressed more frequently than ever. However, it is hard for most Chinese people to adjust to this new way of thinking and find a balance.

One of my business partners is a self-made industrial guru in China. His credo is to treat everyone like his own family, and he prioritises others' interests over himself. Over the past decades, he and his family have regularly visited his employees' families during the Chinese New Year. This tradition is called 'Bainian'. To Chinese households, the more people that come to Bainian, the better the omen. 'How about your own relatives?' I asked him. 'I organise a banquet and invite all of my relatives to get together at once,' he replied. He is called 'Uncle Guo' by all of his staff. This strong tie of affection within Chinese organisations helped tremendously in gaining loyalty and righteousness amongst the staff.

With government authorities, it is another story. Resource allocation is often a thorny problem. For instance, arable land per capita in China is one of the lowest in the world, and the economy relies hugely on labour intensive manufacturing for which land is required to build factories and associated infrastructure. This leads to a conflict in land use, and there are well publicised examples of 'land grabs' where large corporations or local government seize farm land from villagers for industrial use. For those seeking land for development purposes, the ability to influence officials plays a key role. Therefore, 'Government PR' has become a priority of many businesses.

Furthermore, in China, as long as you have the right to 'approve', you are a 'leader'. Leadership is hierarchical, and is hard to challenge. Leaders are facetiously called 'grandma and mum'. Chinese entrepreneurs call the social intercourse with leaders 'burning incense and worshiping Buddha'. When Alibaba's Jack Ma was asked how to maintain a good relationship with the Chinese government, he answered, 'Be in love, but stay unmarried'.

In order to manage these complicated relationships, more and more foreign companies appoint Chinese or people of Chinese descent to important posts in China. But is this the panacea?

In 2005, Bill Gates was outraged at news that Kai-Fu Lee, vice president of the interactive services division, was leaving Microsoft and joining its rival Google. Lee had successfully established Microsoft Research (MSR), which later became known as MSR Asia, in Beijing from 1998 to 2000. Angry Microsoft sued Google and Lee in a Washington state court. Although a settlement was reached in the end, it embroiled the three parties in a five-month court battle, reportedly involving a total of 12 lawyers.

Thrilled Google compensated Dr Lee with an 'unprecedented' package worth $10 million. In order to 'move to the next chapter in my career', Lee left Google in 2009, and set up his own business in Beijing. So, why did Dr Lee, a hotshot among IT giants, a 'highly intelligent scientist, a leader with high emotional intelligence and good reputation among young Chinese hi-tech talents, Chinese government and public', leave Microsoft? During many interviews in the Chinese media, Dr Lee simply answered, 'Different opinions.' Whereas his former colleagues explained, "Kai Fu always wanted to return to China, and proposed a plan for the Chinese market, but Microsoft did not implement this model. The worst damage was from an argument between Kai-Fu and Gates, during which Gates used profane language.

Why did he resign from Google? Kai-Fu's role was indeed very hard. He had to face tough Google headquarters on one side, while facing the challenges of Google's localisation on the other hand. Google's organisational culture doomed it to suffer from an unusual ordeal in China.

So, here comes the key word, culture!

Many western people pompously reckon that China is westernised, so there is no need to learn Chinese culture. My question is, 'Where is the 'west' in China?' Remember that until 2015, only 5% of Chinese citizens held a passport. Many Chinese people have never even seen a foreigner!

Among those 5% of Chinese people, a few inevitably became 'banana-like' (yellow outside, but white inside). But many are like Dr Lee, and have a 'China knot' in their hearts. Therefore, be aware of Chinese culture and of cultural differences and sensitivities. The ability to understand and respond to each culture's strengths and weaknesses is the ultimate key to build and retain relationships.

For example, western psychological theory proposes six primary human emotions, while Chinese idiom describes 'seven emotions and six desires'.

This emphasis on emotional aspects, plus a sense of intimate clan and clique, inform and influence Chinese people's sensitivity and consciousness in relationships, including business relationships. In some ways, managing relationships in China is a matter of 'minding the emotions'.

For many Chinese business partners, a strategic exit strategy is lacking. This is often a result of a 'chivalric spirit', 'If we are not friends, then we will be enemies'. So, when partnerships dissolve, the hurt of sentiment may be greater than that of monetary loss. I believe that, for Chinese business, adopting a more hard-headed western rationale can help to alleviate this problem.

So, managing a relationship is like managing a marriage, understanding each other is the key and this cannot rely on interventions by a mediator or messenger. Doing business in China relies heavily on personal interaction and networking, do not underestimate the importance of these factors and do take the time to foster good relations with your Chinese counterparts.

# Chapter 6
## Selling to Chinese Customers

No matter how wonderful your product, if nobody wants to buy it, it will just become a dust collector. Because of the differences in consumer psychology, motivation and habits, different approaches are needed for Chinese customers.

The pathway to Chinese customers' wallets is through their hearts. As we discussed in the last chapter, Chinese consumers' decisions are predominantly informed by emotions.

The power of love is the key to all successful marketing and sales, especially in a buyer's market. One good example is De Beers Diamond Jewellers; we all know its 'Slogan of the Century' 'A diamond is forever'. When it came to China, this slogan was coloured by emotion and became, 'a diamond is timeless, my love is forever.'

As Chinese are now the largest spenders on international tourism worldwide, training in skills and knowledge about 'Selling to Chinese Customers' has been much in demand by luxury retailers globally. When salespeople confront Chinese clients, the challenges are self-evident: how to interact effectively given the language difficulty, dealing with price negotiations, overcoming emotional annoyance, how to keep in touch, and many other things. Whether a transaction is successful or not, proceeds quickly or slowly and goes as the salesperson expects, may depend not on one big thing, but many small things. An inappropriate gesture or facial expression, an intonation, an inauspicious number or colour can all cause displeasure, even offence. After staff attend a dedicated workshop focused on cultural awareness and behavioural adjustment, the majority of companies find they enjoy increased sales and save appreciable sums on discounts.

To greet Chinese tourists at your own door is a lot easier than to sell in China. The majority of overseas Chinese tourists have one clear purpose; to buy, buy, buy! They spend 75% of their travel budget on shopping, they have limited time, and they normally buy multiple items. Some London West End salespeople said to me, 'When I see a Chinese tour coach parked near my store, I know that I'll reach my sales target.'

In China, the competition is fiercer. There you are not only facing local rivals, but also an influx of international firms. Due to the distinctive political system, socio-economic, social structure and consumer psychology and habits, Chinese business characteristics differ from those in the rest of the world in many aspects, such as business models, brand building tools, marketing strategies, distribution channels, selling techniques, pace setting and many more. Hereafter let's look at some typical Chinese conventional business practices and explain the implicit meanings behind them.

**The 4th class enterprises sell products, the 3rd class enterprises sell services, the 2nd class enterprises sell cultures, the 1st class enterprises sell stories.**

Some stories go in one ear, and out of the other; some go to the head; while some go to the heart. There are over 1300 Chinese characters and words containing 'heart', whereas no more than 40 characters and words contain the word 'brain'. In China the most cherished of the 'golden hearts' is the heart of filial piety (i.e. respect for parents and elders).

On April 16, 2013, Financial Times website published an article entitled *'Tears, reality TV and the Chinese dream'*. It noted that the China MasterChef winning contestant's tear-jerking story helped her secure victory in the final. *"Before the final cook-off, she appeared on stage flanked by her mother, who is dying of end-stage liver disease. 'My illness cannot be cured without a liver transplant ... but I cannot afford one,' her mother told the judges, adding that Ms Zhao had offered to donate half her own liver to save her. 'My dream is to win the championship to get the prize money for my mother's medical treatment'... a debate broke out over whether the competition had been decided by cooking skill or by the sob story."*

This article interested me not because the event itself, but by how it surprised the western writer. To Chinese people, this is normal. Brownie points, sympathy votes, consolation prizes and encouragement awards are widely accepted in many Chinese fields. This debate was just like ripples after a breeze.

In recent years, 'warm', 'inspirational' and 'positive energy' are the key words in story-telling. For the young 'netizens', imaginative and creative story telling also means to spin negatives into positives. For foreign businesses, winning the 'heart of China' is the paramount goal.

**Customers are our Gods; they are always correct. If they are wrong, please refer to the above.**

This sign can be easily found in many Chinese stores. You may have heard lots about the importance of 'Face', here comes some advice on how to give Chinese people 'Face': never offend them. How to achieve this then? Easy! In Chinese the words, customer, client, buyer, shopper, visitor, tourist and passenger, all equate to 'Guest', I believe that you know how to be a host. When hosting a dinner, we will always consider our guests' favourite foods and their dislikes and allergies, because we don't want only to satisfy them, we want to delight them. An awareness of etiquette and taboo, and asking appropriate questions to find customers' needs and preferences is the key.

It's also very important to be completely truthful about products and prices; failure to disclose information about goods or services may also cause annoyance or offence to your clients; after all, you wouldn't like it either!

You may also hear lots about 'Hierarchy' and feel intimidated, but in retail, this is more a psychological suggestion than a cultural phenomenon. Imagine, you are received by the Queen, you have to follow prescribed etiquette, even though you are the guest; while if the Queen is visiting your offices you will also have to be perfectly prepared, even though you are the host. Chinese customers are not gods, nor the Queen, they are an approachable family-oriented nation. They appreciate respect, but they don't like 'boundaries'.

Therefore, there are three steps to gaining long term loyal customers. First, be humble and respectful; second, be knowledgeable, professional and good-humoured; third, behave as if you're a valued or family friend. Once you are friends, there will be very few don'ts or taboos.

**If you dislike it, please tell me; If you do like it, please tell your friends.**

This was a sign created by a Chinese lady in the 1930's and displayed in Chinese couplets in her Shanghai restaurant. Many modern western marketers or advertisers insist on the power of 'word of mouth' and 'peer pressure', but I thought that these couplets were much more intriguing.

During the wartime era, what did this young divorced mother experience? Some gangsters came into her restaurant to dine and dash (i.e. leave without paying). She approached them when they next came in, chatted with them and paid their bill herself. Soon after that the 'God of Shanghai', the leader of the infamous and powerful Green Gang visited her, and from then on there were no more 'dine and dash' incidents. This lady later established the first Chinese five-star hotel.

These days of course, word of mouth includes online sites too. Today in China the online 'Friends Circle', (Peng You Quan), is a very effective tool for spreading the word and influencing people.

### Applying 'Tai Ji' at the negotiation table

I have been asked numerous times about how to deal with Chinese customers' price negotiations, regardless of whether it is in a retail store, an Original Equipment Manufacturer (OEM) quotation or a consultancy service. Sometimes a deal can be killed off over a few pence.

Are Chinese people trapped in the 'hole of the coin'? (Old Chinese coins had a hole in the middle, hence this expression which means to be obsessed by money). Maybe a very few. Think about this, why is gift giving such a huge business in China? Whom are the gifts for? Once a UK luxury watch salesperson told me a memorable story. His client bought several watches, and gave one to the tour guide. At first the tour guide felt embarrassed and wouldn't accept it, however the client was extremely persistent and in the end the guide did accept the gift. Other sales people have told me, 'Chinese customers are very grateful, if you treat them well, they tend to buy more.'

So, if you feel that your Chinese counterparts have been tough on price negotiations, it is very likely because they feel you are an outsider. You can either step back to re-build a closer personal relationship with them, or use the technique of Tai Ji: gently lean backwards, but stand steady and keep to the bottom line. In practice this means to soften your tone, say that you would really like to offer the product at a reduced price, however... (explain how your price came to be set... that you can't go against your company's pricing policy.... that you'd get into trouble with your manager... and so forth), most customers won't keep pushing after three attempts. And lastly, don't take it too seriously. Asking for discount is mostly just habit. When they negotiate a million-pound deal, they'll ask for a discount; when they go to buy a kilo of apples, they still ask for discount. It's a mentality: "I'm doing you a favour, so you should do me a favour in return". This is an opportunity for you to build and strengthen your relationship; engage in some good humoured wrangling, indulge in chit-chat, don't give up too much, and learn to enjoy the process! Just remember that you need a more varied and flexible pricing strategy for your Chinese customers. For example, using the Chinese lucky number 8 in pricing and negotiations is often a good idea (never underestimate the power of superstition when you're dealing with China).

Emotions and logic are indispensable to each other. Without passion, nothing will be started; without logic, nothing will end perfectly.

# Chapter 7
## Localisation or Globalisation?

'Unacclimatised' is the most common word used by Chinese people to comment on foreign companies' failure in China. Many of these companies have a lifespan in China of less than two years. In this chapter, we will discuss how to acclimatise yourself to the new environment.

'Think global, act local' is easy to say, but it's hard to implement, isn't it? A Chinese story tells of a plain country girl who dreamed of attracting people's admiration like a far-famed beauty from a neighbouring village. One day, she encountered the beauty and saw her walking stooped, with arms crossed over her chest and with her eyebrows knitted. Emulating the beauty's posture, she walked around her village, but the villagers were alarmed rather than admiring. In fact, the beauty had been suffering from chest pains that day. This tale illustrates that an inappropriate imitation often produces an opposite effect to that intended.

In September 2014, GlaxoSmithKline China Investment Ltd. (GSKCI) was fined ¥3 billion (£297m) by the Chinese authorities on the grounds of bribery. Mark Reilly, British former executive of the company was sentenced to 3 years in prison. What he had done was request that all his sales people attend a two-week 'Public Relationship' training course before starting work, and grant each of them a ¥10,000 'social allowance' together with a list of clients' personal information, including details of their family members and hobbies. This is quite common in China, and the amount of money was not huge. But the problem was that Mr. Reilly broke the unspoken rule, he systemised it into an organisational procedure. Where there is a game, there are rules, play it well!

In addition to considering localisation or globalisation, I would also suggest trying to integrate strengths and find ways of building on complementary cultural characteristics. Here are some points for consideration.

### Relationships

Relationships are crucial. Within an organisation, there are shareholders, a management team and employees. Surrounding it there are business partners, suppliers and customers, and beyond is government, media and the wider community. Successful Chinese business leaders know how to stimulate loyalty and 'buy-in' from their staff and customers.

In 2012, Dalian Wanda acquired AMC Theatres for $2.6 billion. Before the acquisition, AMC had losses in three consecutive years. When Mr Wang took leadership he kept all the US management team and announced his new policy: this was to allow another three years of loss, after which the staff would share 10% of any profits with the company. The result was that the company turned into profit the first year. You may also have heard that in 2015, Chinese Tiens Group treated 6,400 employees to a tour of France at a cost of €13 million. This was not a unique grandstand show, but a demonstration of the family values and sense of sharing underpinning Chinese culture, including businesses. In Chinese, the word 'country' literally means 'national family'; we regard our own household as the small family, the organisation is the second family and the country is our big family.

As a foreigner in China, having an understanding of Chinese national sentiment is vital. A foreign company received massive levels of protest from Chinese consumers because they had 'Made in Republic of Taiwan' printed on their packaging. To Mainland Chinese, Taiwan is regarded as an integral part of the People's Republic of China. Any suggestion that it is independent causes grave insult and offence. This kind of negligence could easily kill off your business prospects in China.

## Products

I was once asked to help with importing some coffee machines into China, but the supplier refused to do a deal. The reason was that the water in the particular area China was too hard and the pipes in the coffee machines are easily blocked. But, the buyer did not want to spend extra money on installing water filters. This was a really wise decision on the part of the supplier. To prevent a crisis is much more cost effective than trying to solve it.

It is also worth noting that, contrary to popular opinion, things are not always badly made in China. For example, if you're selling kitchens in China, it's a good idea to use Chinese made cooker hoods. They generally work better and last longer as they are designed to cope with the heavy smoke generated by traditional Chinese stir-fry cooking methods.

## Organisational Culture

'A book should be written in the reader's language; trains need to run on the same tracks.' Cultural integration is the key lynchpin of merged companies. For multinational companies, both national culture and corporate culture need to be harmoniously fused. Otherwise the intended result of '1+1>2' (the whole is greater than the sum of the parts) will instead end up in 'Two turkeys do not make an Eagle'.

In 2005, the Taiwanese BenQ Corp. acquired German Siemens Mobile and formed BenQ-Siemens. In this acquisition, Siemens handed over € 250 million in assets. After only 18 months, BenQ-Siemens went bankrupt with losses of € 800 million. Similar tragedies or unhappy marriages include China's TCL communication and French Alcatel's TAMP, Chinese Wahaha and French Danone, and many others.

On investigation of the reasons for these failures, many insiders admitted that culture was the foremost reason, and it manifests itself at three levels.

Firstly, the national characteristics; these are deeply influenced by Yin-Yang ideology, in which everything in the world is a unity of opposites, and where these two confrontational properties constantly move and interact with each other. This movement and interaction decide the world's growth, development and ending. Chinese people tend to be changeable in mind and resilient in action. Their decision making is mainly based on friends' opinions rather than expert advice. Once a decision is made, they like speedy execution, this is often referred to as 'China Speed'. 'The devil is the detail' isn't applicable for Chinese people. Then, when things have gone wrong, they make a quick exit.

Is this good or bad? Both! Take the example of BenQ-Siemens. Chinese consumers' handset replacement cycle has always been ranking top worldwide. BenQ wanted swift product upgrading, which the more technically rigorous Germans found hard to accept and implement. Conflict between marketers and technicians became inevitable. However, fast speed is often incompatible with good quality, and that's why the average lifespan of Chinese enterprises is relatively shorter than that of western ones.

On the other hand, German products have built up a reputation for good build quality and reliability, as a result, 'made in Germany' has become a stamp of trustworthiness.

Secondly, the vast majority of Chinese companies are entrepreneurial. 'New born calves are not afraid of tigers'; they seek any and all opportunities for success. Their rapid, multiple expansion ambitions can take off any time. On the other hand, many established western companies are fiscally conservative and systematic. Careful assessment and limitation of risk is a major consideration. In addition, Chinese corporate structures, salary systems and sales models are all different to foreign ones.

Thirdly, people. When teams are formed from people speaking different languages, factions are naturally created. On most occasions, English is the common communication language. You know what? We tease that 'Chinglish talks to Frenlish or Xxlish'. I have heard that a Spaniard understood 'Cappuccino' as 'a cup of tea'; I was even told that an English person mis-heard an American's 'rest room' as 'restaurant'.

Also be aware of sensitivities: when a British manager in Shanghai kindly tried to provide coaching for one of her Chinese staff in order to ready him for promotion he got very upset about it. He completely misunderstood her motive; in his eyes the coach was engaged to correct shortcomings in his performance.

Some companies think that simply hiring some Mandarin speaking staff will solve the problem at a stroke. But the reality is often disappointing, as it just papers over the cracks. I have trained many mixed teams of Chinese and other nationalities. All enjoyed the course. I once presented at a big brand's annual conference. There were about eighty managers from different countries and regions. At the very beginning, I asked, 'Who has shaken a Chinese customer's hand?' Only one raised her hand. I asked, 'Where are you from?' 'China', she answered. All the people in the boardroom laughed. Some HR directors and managers have also asked me, 'We have some Chinese staff, but they often ask for sick leave, what can I do?'

The solution to the 'people' issue is all about global leadership and international professionalism. Success can be achieved by a programme focused on opening communication channels, and promoting mutual understanding, respect and trust. For example, in the case of the company experiencing high sickness rates the answer is to set clear, documented rules and limits, in the contractual conditions of employment for all staff, on the amount of paid ad hoc sick leave that's allowable. Transgressions should result in clearly understood consequences, such as loss of pay and ultimately dismissal. Of course, real cases of chronic illness should be treated fairly and sympathetically, we're only trying to discourage slackers, not penalise people who are genuinely sick.

In the case of the company where only their Chinese employee had engaged with Chinese customers there was clear need to broaden the scope of contact. What happened when she was on holiday, did they just leave their customers waiting until she got back? How would they cope if she left the company? And, do you think it's good business practice to distance yourself from customers in this way. By all means let your Chinese employees advise you, lead negotiations where necessary and smooth the path, but do remember that Chinese culture is all about personal contacts and relationships and there's really no substitute for your personal involvement.

Of course, the influence from politics, the media and society at large also needs to be taken into account. But people are the creators and custodians of all cultures; we are wonderfully adaptable to cultural differences and perfectly capable of creating a sustainable and nurturing 'blended culture'. All we need is to be open minded, curious about new things and willing to learn.

# Chapter 8
## Sustainable Win-Win-Win


Confucius said, 'Wealth and honours are what men desire. If they cannot be obtained in a just and ethical way, they should not be held. Poverty and meanness are what men dislike. If they cannot be avoided in a just and ethical way, they should not be avoided.' A common Chinese phrase says, 'True gentlemen make their wealth in proper ways.' That's why the adult, gambling and drug trafficking industries are regarded as 'three vices' and resolutely prohibited in modern Mainland China. Of course these things are common, but punishments can be very severe indeed with long custodial sentences being handed down, and trafficking in hard drugs could attract capital punishment. Also, influenced by Confucianism and Taoism, a 'morality courtroom' has arisen amongst sections of the public and the on-line community. The behaviour of celebrities, officials and businesses is subject to public scrutiny and criticism, and adverse comment can result in severe reputational and business loss. Successful and ethical businessmen are hailed as 'ru shang' (Confucian businessman).

Regarding the consistency of Chinese ideology and philosophy, it is noteworthy that the Chinese character for 'profit' contains a knife which hints at violence. The English word interest means benefit, profit and hobby or attraction. In the current extremely competitive era, striking the right balance of people, place, products and productivity, price and profit is getting more and more complex and difficult. Recently, I heard a delegate at our Leadership master class asking, 'Is tax avoidance ethical, it is not illegal.' I said, 'If all the businesses in this country avoid tax, what will happen?' Simply, a sole win for an individual or company is not necessarily a real win in a larger socio-economic context.

On 17 March 2013, newly elected Chinese Chairman Xi Jinping proposed the 'China Dream' in his Government Work Report. Soon after, the Silk Road Economic Belt and the 21st-Century Maritime Silk Road (the Belt and Road) were initiated. The Chinese people clearly understand that regional stability is the foundation of China's rejuvenation dream. The former Australian Prime Minister Kevin Rudd endorsed the China Dream as mankind's dream during a Ted Talk speech in 2015.

The Belt and Road is an Economic Cooperation Framework, including road network construction, trade flow, currency circulation, internet development and other mutually beneficial bilateral and multilateral mechanisms. In 2015, China directly invested USD1.2 billion in 49 associate countries. In January 2016, the Asian Infrastructure Investment Bank (AIIB) was launched. The United Nations has declared that AIIB has the potential for 'scaling up financing for sustainable development'.

While opening the international trade channels, the Chinese government's domestic priority is eradicating poverty and improving people's livelihood. The goal is that by 2020, a further seventy million people will be raised out of poverty. Improvements in infrastructure, housing, health care, education, public facilities and services are planned for many of China's less developed regions, together with many industries that are seen in the west as 'sunset'. Anything beneficial to China's development and growth, will also benefit the enterprises themselves. Jack Ma's motivation for Alibaba was to help Chinese SMEs to go global. He said, 'If I could help them to become richer, I will be richer.'

Let's take a look at the Danone and Wahaha case. In 1996, Danone acquired a 51% stake in Wahaha, and pocketed 5 fold profits from the joint venture in the next ten years. But Mr. Zong Qinghou, the founder and chairman of Wahaha Group was not happy in this marriage. Not only because Danone's elaborately designed partnership agreement became a serious impediment to his business execution, but also Danone kept acquiring other rivals to provoke price competition.

In 1999, in response to the Chinese government's initiative of 'Development of the Western Areas' and 'Counterpart Support of Old Revolutionary Base Areas', Mr. Zong proposed a business expansion plan to the western areas of China, but was refused by Danone on the grounds that the spending power in these poorer and relatively undeveloped areas was low. Therefore, Mr. Zong set up some Chinese capital only companies and operated them under the Wahaha brand. By 2006, these companies were making an attractive profit. Envious Danone tried to acquire the remainder of Wahaha at a very low cost but this move was strongly resisted by Mr Zong. Although Danone technically had the upper hand, after 29 trials in courts around the globe, and personal interventions by both former French president Sarkozy and Chinese chairman Hu Jintao, Danone lost the case. Eventually a settlement was reached in Stockholm, under which Wahaha bought back all the stocks from the Joint Venture at a reasonable price.

In this commercial 'battle of the century', Danone were labelled 'greedy predators' by the Chinese public. They lost both their wished for profit and (in China at least) their reputation.

Although China has made enormous progress and incredible socio-economic achievements since 1978, the price has been very high, not only in terms of environmental damage, the most visible of which is the notorious pollution problem; but also damage to humanity, e.g. the disappearance of natural, traditional villages and the huge increase in marginalized urban populations. These problems occurred widely, because the rapid poverty reduction and accumulation of wealth were impeded by a lack of knowledge, skills, tools and equipment.

Sustainable development in China is not only about a healthy ecological and spiritual system, but also has a great pragmatic significance. There are lessons to be learned for potential investors. Let me share two stories here.

When a British car maker entered the Chinese market they designed a new look model for Chinese consumers, featuring a re-designed exterior and a lavish interior. So far, so good: but then they decided that to save on costs the new model should comply only with the Chinese exhaust emission criteria which are much less stringent than those in the UK. Quality control was also poor. However, the price was kept high, equivalent to that in the UK. Soon after those cars came onto the road, problems with engine stalling and the gear box occurred. Frustrated users grumbled that the car was a 'Road Blocking Tiger' and voiced their discontent online.

As a consequence, its shortcomings were exposed on the very popular China CCTV's annual '3.15' Consumer Rights TV Show, which targets companies for shoddy products, injustices and violations. In response the company stated that; 'We offer our sincere apologies for any inconvenience and concern this may have caused our customers', and began to offer software and gearbox updates to correct the issues.

This programme's impact is tremendous: exposed companies will not only lose their credibility, but also will be shortlisted for attention by the authorities and enforcement agencies.

A diametrically opposite example is that of the Shandong Zaozhuang Hanro Winery Co. Ltd. This Chinese / German Cooperative's name 'Hanro' came from German winemaker Norbert Gorres (1934-2009) and his assistant Hans Beu (1947-2007), who were eulogized by Chinese President Xi Jinping in a speech during his visit to Germany in 2014.

In 2000, invited by the SAFEA (State Administration of Foreign Experts Affairs of China), Norbert and Hans arrived in Zaozhuang to help local farmers with viticulture and grafting. Zaozhuang was once claimed as a 'coal capital' and 'fruit base'. With the depletion of coal reserves the local government was seeking industrial transformation, ideally ecological agriculture. But this plan was hindered by real problems such as ageing plant varieties, ineffective disease and pest control, a lack of technical expertise and poor management. With hands on assistance from Norbert and Hans, local farmers successfully cultivated German grape varieties within three years. At this point, people thought that Norbert and Hans' job was done.

But they came back, firstly because they could not forget the locals, they had treated them so kindly and sincerely; secondly, when Norbert read a German newspaper saying that tens of millions of Chinese farmers had to leave their home towns for cities in order to make a living, an idea came into his mind. He proposed that a local coal mining company set up a winery, and he would provide technical support and authorise use of his family owned wine label. In 2006, Hanro Winery Co. Ltd. was born.

While commuting between Germany and Zaozhuang, Norbert and Hans also subsidised schooling for eight underprivileged Chinese students. Just before Hans died from cancer in 2007, he asked Norbert to deliver a final donation from him to the children. In memory of these two experts, a local road is also named Hanro, and a two-meter-high bronze statue of Norbert stands in the vineyard. He was awarded 'The People's Republic of China Friendship Award', which is the highest award for 'foreign experts who have made outstanding contributions to the country's economic and social progress'.

Today, Hanro's vineyard has expanded to about 50,000 acres, and produces 600,000 liters of wine with a turnover ¥150 million per year. Local farmers' income has doubled or even tripled. The vineyard itself became an AAAA tourism attraction. Norbert's grandson, Marc Linden is now following in grandfather's footsteps to help Hanro become a world class winery.

The word 'Generous' in Chinese consists of 'Giving' and 'Gaining'. A Chinese idiom says. 'If you receive the favour of a drop of water, you should return it with a flowing spring'.

# Conclusion

I have met many business people who are interested in expanding into China. But what stops them? Well, mostly it's fear: fear of the unknown. I hope that this Bite-Sized Book will help you start to 'know' China, and will remove some of the fear factors. I have heard some of my trainees saying: 'After all, we are all human beings.' Exactly! So be open, embrace differences and believe in humanity's excellent adaptability. A Chinese classic poem says, 'Stones from other hills may serve to polish the jade of this one'. If you have a China dream, please chase it. 'If you are bright, China will never be dark.'

China is the world's oldest continuous civilisation. Its rich culture still has much to reveal and offer to the west. I believe that by expanding your business into China, you will also help bring your culture to China. By so doing, you will contribute to China, to your home country and to the global community.

The Chinese philosopher Xunzi said, 'A journey of thousands of miles may not be achieved through the accumulation of each single step.' I understand that your journey to China has so many tasks to get through. In order to help you to understand China better I am planning to write a series of Bite-Sized Books to provide information in more scope and depth. If you have any suggestions, ideas or stories to share with me (and with a wider audience), please feel free to contact me. It would be very much appreciated!

Thank you for reading this book and all the best!

BITE-SIZED
BOOKS

**Bite-Sized Business Books** are designed to provide support and insights for professionals who are tackling an unfamiliar task either for the first time or after a gap, as well as those who want to find new ways of doing what they are familiar with.

They are deliberately short, easy to read, step-by-step manuals and books guiding the reader through the various stages behind each business process or activity, with a clear focus on outcomes. They are firmly based on personal experience and success.

The most successful people all share an ability to focus on what really matters, keeping things simple and understandable. MBAs, metrics and methodologies have their place, but when we are faced with a new challenge most of us need quick guidance on what matters most, from people who have been there before and who can show us where to start. As Stephen Covey famously said, "The main thing is to keep the main thing, the main thing".

But what exactly is the main thing?

Bite-Sized books were conceived to help answer precisely that question crisply and fast and, of course, be engaging to read, written by people who are experienced and successful in their field.

The brief? Distil the "main things" into a book that can be read by an intelligent non-expert comfortably in around 60 minutes. Make sure the book enables the reader with specific tools, ideas and plenty of examples drawn from real life and business. Be a virtual mentor.

Bite-Sized Books don't cover every eventuality, but they are written from the heart by successful people who are happy to share their experience with you and give you the benefit of their success.

We have avoided jargon – or explained it where we have used it as a shorthand – and made few assumptions about the reader, except that they are in business, are literate and numerate, and that they can adapt and use what we suggest to suit their own, individual purposes. Whether you are working for a multi-national corporation or a start-up or something in between, the principles we introduce will hold good.

They can be read straight through at one easy sitting and then used as a support while you are working on what you need to do.

BITE-SIZED
BOOKS

# Bite-Sized Books Catalogue

## Business Books

**Ian Benn**
    **Write to Win**
        **How to Produce Winning Proposals and RFP Responses**

**Matthew T Brown**
    **Understand Your Organisation**
        **An Introduction to Enterprise Architecture Modelling**

**David Cotton**
    **Rethinking Leadership**
        **Collaborative Leadership for Millennials and Beyond**

**Richard Cribb**
    **IT Outsourcing: 11 Short Steps to Success**
        **An Insider's View**

**Phil Davies**
    **How to Survive and Thrive as a Project Manager**
        **The Guide for Successful Project Managers**

**Paul Davies**
    **Developing a Business Case**
        **Making a Persuasive Argument out of Your Numbers**

**Paul Davies**
    **Developing a Business Plan**
        **Making a Persuasive Case for Your Business**

Paul Davies
    Contract Management for Non-Specialists
Paul Davies
    Developing Personal Effectiveness in Business
Paul Davies
    A More Effective Sales Team
        Sales Management Focused on Sales People
Tim Emmett
    Bid for Success
        Building the Right Strategy and Team
Nigel Greenwood
    Why You Should Welcome Customer Complaints
        And What to Do About Them
Nigel Greenwood
    Six Things that All Customer Want
        A Practical Guide to Delivering Simply Brilliant
        Customer Service
Ian Hucker
    Risk Management in IT Outsourcing
        9 Short Steps to Success
Marcus Lopes and Carlos Ponce
    Retail Wars
        May the Mobile be with You
Maiqi Ma
    Win with China
        Acclimatisation for Mutual Success Doing Business
        with China
Elena Mihajloska
    Bridging the Virtual Gap
        Building Unity and Trust in Remote Teams
Rob Morley
    Agile in Business
        A Guide for Company Leadership
Gillian Perry
    Managing the People Side of Change
        Ten Short Steps to Success in IT Outsourcing

Saibal Sen
>Next Generation Service Management
>>An Analytics Driven Approach

Don Sharp
>Nothing Happens Until You Sell Something
>>A Personal View of Selling Techniques

## Lifestyle Books

Anna Corthout
>Alive Again
>>My Journey to Recovery

Phil Davies
>Don't Worry  Be Happy
>>A Personal Journey

Phil Davies
>Feel the Fear and Pack Anyway
>>Around the World in 284 Days

Regina Kerschbaumer
>Yoga Coffee and a Glass of Wine
>>A Yoga Journey

Arthur Worrell
>A Grandfather's Story
>>Arthur Worrell's War

## Public Affairs Books

Eben Black
>Lies Lunch and Lobbying
>>PR, Public Affairs and Political Engagement – A Guide

Christian Wolmar
>Wolmar for London
>>Creating a Grassroots Campaign in a Digital Age

www.ingramcontent.com/pod-product-compliance
Lightning Source LLC
Chambersburg PA
CBHW071545170526
45166CB00004B/1565